RollingStone

ROCK TRIVIA

CHALLENGE

Published by Sellers Publishing, Inc.

Copyright © 2020 Sellers Publishing, Inc.

Content © 2020 Rolling Stone, LLC

Rolling Stone is a registered trademark of Rolling Stone LLC.

Used under license. All rights reserved.

Sellers Publishing, Inc.

161 John Roberts Road, South Portland, Maine 04106

Visit our website: www.sellerspublishing.com • E-mail: rsp@rsvp.com

Charlotte Cromwell, Production Editor

ISBN 13: 978-1-5319-1221-5

10 9 8 7 6 5 4 3 2 1

Printed and bound in United States of America.

RollingStone

ROCK TRIVIA

CHALLENGE

Test Your Rock Music Knowledge

SELLERS
PUBLISHING

RollingStone

ROCK TRIVIA CHALLENGE

How many **GRATEFUL DEAD** keyboardists
(or former keyboardists) died during the 1980s?

(A) 1

(B) 2

(C) 3

(D) 4

Answer: (A) 1. R.I.P. Keith Godchaux, who died in
1980; Ronald "Pigpen" McKernan died in 1973;
Brent Mydland in 1990; Vince Welnick in 2006.
Fare thee well, fare thee well.

Why did **BUDDY HOLLY** fail his military medical exam?

(A) Bad eyesight

(B) Flat feet

(C) Bad hearing

(D) Fear of flying

Who kicked off the hip-hop craze for
JAMES BROWN samples with the 1987 single
"I Know You Got Soul"?

(A) Eric B. and Rakim

(B) Public Enemy

(C) Mantronix

(D) Stetsasonic

"WAR," the song written by Norman Whitfield and Barrett Strong and later recorded by Bruce Springsteen, was first recorded by which **MOTOWN** act?

(A) The Temptations

(B) The Four Tops

(C) Martha and the Vandellas

(D) Edwin Starr

What was Bob Dylan's nickname on the first
TRAVELING WILBURYS record?

(A) Nelson Wilbury

(B) Lucky Wilbury

(C) Boo Wilbury

(D) Spike Wilbury

(E) Bob Wilbury

Answer: (B) Lucky Wilbury. He called himself Boo
Wilbury on the second album.

Abstract expressionist artist **ROBERT RAUSCHENBERG** won a Grammy for the limited-edition cover he designed for which Talking Heads album?

(A) *Remain in Light*

(B) *Speaking in Tongues*

(C) *Stop Making Sense*

(D) *The Name of This Band Is Talking Heads*

If you're a member of soft-rock duo **AIR SUPPLY**, why might you be suffering from headaches?

(A) Because you're bangin' your head on the side of the bed

(B) Because you're lyin' alone with your head on the phone

(C) Because the voices in your head are makin' you see red

(D) Because your head's on the floor and your heart's out the door

Answer: (B) Because you're lyin' alone with your head on the phone

"Does anybody know about the **QUAKE**?"

(A) "Yeah!"

(B) "Hell, yeah!"

(C) "Yeah! Bullshit!"

(D) "Only the sexy people!"

Answer: (C) "Yeah! Bullshit!" The line is from 1987's "Housequake."

11

How did **ROCKWELL** get Michael Jackson to sing the hook on "Somebody's Watching Me"?

(A) They met at a Jehovah's Witnesses meeting

(B) He was dating Michael's sister Janet

(C) He was working as Michael's chauffeur

(D) He was Motown founder Berry Gordy's son

In 1988, when the Beatles were inducted into the **ROCK AND ROLL HALL OF FAME**, George Harrison said, "There were only two real fifth Beatles." Whom did he mention?

(A) Stu Sutcliffe and Pete Best

(B) George Martin and Brian Epstein

(C) Derek Taylor and Neil Aspinall

(D) Murray the K and Phil Spector

Answer: (C) Derek Taylor and Neil Aspinall. Taylor was the Beatles' public relations manager, and Aspinall was the band's road manager who later became chief executive of Apple Corps.

13

The last performer at Woodstock was **JIMI HENDRIX**, who took the stage on Monday morning. How many of the estimated 400,000 concertgoers on hand at the height of the festival stuck around to hear Hendrix?

(A) 400,000

(B) 200,000

(C) 100,000

(D) 25,000

Answer: (D) 25,000

Who are the **JUGGALOS**, and where do they gather each summer?

(A) Fans of the String Cheese Incident who gather in Boulder, Colorado

(B) A group of dance music fans who gather at the Detroit Electronic Music Festival

(C) Devotees of Insane Clown Posse who gather at a giant festival in the Midwest

(D) Phish-loving jugglers who gather at Phish shows

According to "**MATERIAL GIRL**,"
what kind of boy is always Mr. Right?

(A) Boys who save their pennies

(B) Boys with the cold hard cash

(C) Boys who give her proper credit

(D) Boys who kiss and hug her

Answer: (B) Boys with the cold hard cash

Which **MEL BROOKS MOVIE** inspired the title for U2's album *Achtung Baby*?

(A) *Young Frankenstein*

(B) *Blazing Saddles*

(C) *The Producers*

(D) *Silent Movie*

Match the "**PENNY LANE**"
character with what he does

(A) Banker

(B) Fireman

(C) Nurse

(D) Barber

(1) Keeps a portrait of the queen in his pocket

(2) Collects photographs of his clients

(3) Never wears appropriate rain gear

(4) Peddles flowers in urban traffic

Answer: (A-3), (B-1), (C-4), (D-2)

Which of the following did **JERRY LEE LEWIS** not do?

(A) Finance a trip to Sun Studios by selling 33 dozen eggs

(B) Study at a Pentecostal academy

(C) Marry his teenage cousin

(D) Record an album of gospel duets with his cousin Jimmy Lee Swaggart

Which movie featured **BILL HALEY AND HIS COMETS'** "Rock Around the Clock," propelling the song to Number One?

(A) *The Night of the Hunter*

(B) *Rebel Without a Cause*

(C) *Blackboard Jungle*

(D) *Abbott and Costello Meet the Mummy*

Answer: (C) *Blackboard Jungle*

For which guitarist did **STEVIE WONDER** originally write "Superstition"?

(A) Eric Clapton

(B) Jeff Beck

(C) Jimi Hendrix

(D) Richard Thompson

Which song with a stuttering vocal performance by **RANDY BACHMAN** of Bachman-Turner Overdrive was intended to poke fun at his speech-impaired brother, Gary?

(A) "No Sugar Tonight"

(B) "American Woman"

(C) "Takin' Care of Business"

(D) "You Ain't Seen Nothing Yet"

Answer: (D) "You Ain't Seen Nothing Yet," by Bachman-Turner Overdrive, was originally intended as a prank single with just one copy, for Gary. After it hit Number One around the world, Bachman has said, "Gary stopped stuttering."

Line from a Led Zeppelin song, or excerpt from
BELL BIV DEVOE's 1990 hit "Do Me!"?

(A) "Squeeze me, baby, till the juice runs down my leg"

(B) "Backstage, underage, adolescent"

(C) "Your custard pie, I declare, it's sweet and nice"

(D) "You say your body's aching? I know that it's aching"

(E) "Take off your clothes and leave on your shoes"

Answer: (A) Led Zeppelin, from "The Lemon Song," (B) "Do Me!,"
(C) Led Zeppelin, from "Custard Pie," (D) Led Zeppelin,
from "Wearing and Tearing," (E) "Do Me!"

23

What sport are they playing at the picnic in
"NUTHIN' BUT A 'G' THANG"?

(A) Basketball

(B) Volleyball

(C) Tennis

(D) Football

Answer: (B) Volleyball

98 DEGREES' 1999 hit "I Do (Cherish You)" was originally

(A) A country song

(B) Written by Prince

(C) A Fifties doo-wop song

(D) Rejected by the Backstreet Boys

When **SAM COOKE** left the gospel group the Highway Q.C.s, who took his place?

(A) Brook Benton

(B) Lou Rawls

(C) Marvin Gaye

Answer: (B) Lou Rawls

All the following fictional characters are referenced
in the **BRUCE SPRINGSTEEN** song
"I'm a Rocker" except

(A) Kojak

(B) Batman

(C) Columbo

(D) Superman

In the Rolling Stones' classic "**(I CAN'T GET NO) SATISFACTION**," Mick Jagger's TV-watching experience is ruined when a man comes on and tells him

(A) How clean his floor can be

(B) How clean his car can be

(C) How white his teeth can be

(D) How white his shirts can be

Answer: (D) How white his shirts can be

Which of the following actors has **NEVER GUEST-STARRED** in a Michael Jackson video?

(A) Wesley Snipes

(B) Marlon Brando

(C) Eddie Murphy

(D) Johnny Depp

Answer: (D) Johnny Depp. Snipes, Brando and Murphy appeared in Jackson's clips for "Bad," "You Rock My World" and "Remember the Time," respectively.

29

For which food or beverage did the
ROLLING STONES record their only
original commercial jingle?

(A) Coca-Cola

(B) Cadbury Chocolate

(C) Heinz Baked Beans

(D) Rice Krispies

Answer: (D) Rice Krispies. It begins, "Wake up in the
morning, there's a snap around the place/Wake up
in the morning, there's a crackle in your face . . ."

Which song was so similar to Radiohead's **"CREEP"** that its authors got a songwriting credit on Radiohead's album *Pablo Honey*?

(A) Steely Dan, "Dr. Wu"

(B) The Hollies, "The Air That I Breathe"

(C) Thunderclap Newman, "Something in the Air"

(D) The Velvet Underground, "New Age"

How did **MIAMI STEVE** get his name?

(A) He's from Miami

(B) He lost big in a bet on the Dolphins

(C) He hates cold weather

(D) He is a fan of the "bass music" scene

Answer: (C) He hates cold weather

With eight weeks at Number One,
what was the **BEE GEES'** biggest hit?

(A) "Stayin' Alive"

(B) "Night Fever"

(C) "You Should Be Dancing"

(D) "Tragedy"

(E) "If I Can't Have You"

(F) "How Deep Is Your Love"

THE CLASH's 1981 album *Sandinista!*
pays tribute to the left-wing revolution in which
Latin American country?

(A) El Salvador

(B) Nicaragua

(C) Guatemala

(D) Honduras

Answer: (B) Nicaragua

Which **EVERLY BROTHERS** single has been covered by Andy Gibb and Victoria Principal, Stephen Colbert and Elvis Costello, and Linda Ronstadt and Kermit the Frog?

(A) "Wake Up Little Susie"

(B) "All I Have to Do Is Dream"

(C) "Bye Bye Love"

(D) "Bird Dog"

What's Johnny doing in the basement in
"SUBTERRANEAN HOMESICK BLUES"?

(A) Thinking about the government

(B) Lighting up the candles

(C) Looking for a new fool

(D) Mixing up the medicine

Answer: (D) Mixing up the medicine

JANET JACKSON became a superstar with the breakup songs on her 1986 album *Control*. The husband she was breaking up with was a member of which family group?

(A) DeBarge

(B) The Sylvers

(C) The Jets

(D) The Jacksons

FATBOY SLIM, the man behind "The Rockafeller Skank," got his start playing bass in which Eighties indie-pop band?

(A) The House of Love

(B) Red House Painters

(C) The Housemartins

(D) Chapterhouse

Answer: (C) The Housemartins

You are a member of **TOTO**, and you are traveling to Africa. What frightens you?

(A) The wild dogs crying in the night

(B) The sight of Mount Kilimanjaro

(C) The realization that love isn't always on time

(D) This thing that you've become

Elvis turned down a starring role in
which film that might have been his
BIG SCREEN COMEBACK?

(A) *A Star Is Born*

(B) *Star Wars*

(C) *Smokey and the Bandit*

(D) *The Godfather, Part II*

Answer: (A) *A Star Is Born.* Elvis turned down a
starring role in the Academy Award-winning
1976 film. The role went to Kris Kristofferson.

Who attempted to call their **DEBUT ALBUM**
*Talking Bear Mountain Picnic Massacre
Disaster Dylan Blues* but were overruled
by their record company?

(A) Genesis

(B) Tony Orlando and Dawn

(C) Procol Harum

(D) Mott the Hoople

In "**PROVE IT ALL NIGHT**,"
Bruce Springsteen is going to teach the girl
all the following sins except

(A) Steal

(B) Cheat

(C) Lie

(D) Kill

Which **PRINCE** song inspired **TIPPER GORE** to found the music censoring group PMRC?

(A) "Darling Nikki"

(B) "Dirty Mind"

(C) "Head"

(D) "Sister"

In "50 Ways to Leave Your Lover," how many methods of lover-leaving does **PAUL SIMON** actually describe?

(A) 5

(B) 8

(C) 25

(D) 50

Which **BLUES SINGER** sued Led Zeppelin in 1985, claiming the group's "Whole Lotta Love" was lifted from his own composition "You Need Love"?

(A) Robert Johnson

(B) Blind Willie Johnson

(C) Willie Dixon

(D) B.B. King

Which song was the theme for the 1985 summer blockbuster *Perfect*, which starred **JOHN TRAVOLTA** as a *ROLLING STONE* writer dating fitness guru Jamie Lee Curtis?

(A) Scritti Politti's "Perfect Way"

(B) Jermaine Jackson's "(Closest Thing to) Perfect"

(C) R.E.M.'s "Perfect Circle"

(D) Hüsker Dü's "Perfect Example"

On which song does **ROD STEWART** encourage you to "let your inhibitions run wild"?

(A) "Hot Legs"

(B) "Maggie May"

(C) "Tonight's the Night (Gonna Be Alright)"

(D) "Do Ya Think I'm Sexy?"

What 1990 album by jokey Eighties punks
THE DEAD MILKMEN took a titular swipe
at a famed Led Zeppelin record?

(A) *The Song Remains Inane*

(B) *Out Through the In Door*

(C) *Souses of the Holy*

(D) *Metaphysical Graffiti*

Answer: (D) *Metaphysical Graffiti*

"Domo arigato, **MR. ROBOTO**"
is Japanese for

(A) "Free me, Mr. Roboto"

(B) "Prepare to die, Mr. Roboto"

(C) "Thank you, Mr. Roboto"

(D) "I need control, Mr. Roboto"

Satiric singer-songwriter **RANDY NEWMAN**'s
1974 release *Good Old Boys* was a
concept album about

(A) Watergate

(B) The South

(C) The oil crisis

(D) Stock-car racing

Answer: (B) The South. Newman even performed a
song written by Huey P. Long.

What did Keith Richards do immediately after coming up with the riff to "**SATISFACTION**"?

(A) Called Mick Jagger and sang it over the phone to him

(B) Shot heroin

(C) Taped it and went back to sleep

(D) Smashed his guitar against the wall

Which of the following songs does not
feature a **MANDOLIN**?

(A) Rod Stewart, "Maggie May"

(B) The Rolling Stones, "Paint It, Black"

(C) Led Zeppelin, "The Battle of Evermore"

(D) The Grateful Dead, "Friend of the Devil"

The "**BILLIE JEAN**" video had the pavement lighting up under Michael Jackson's feet with each step. This was an homage to which famous Hollywood movie-musical number?

(A) "I'll Build a Stairway to Paradise,"
   An American in Paris

(B) "Young and Healthy," *42nd Street*

(C) "Let Me Entertain You," *Gypsy*

(D) "Bonjour, Paris," *Funny Face*

Which band was in the studio to see **JOY DIVISION** record "Love Will Tear Us Apart"?

(A) UB40

(B) U2

(C) The Fall

(D) The Smiths

Answer: (B) U2

Each of these stars attended the same
British school as **ADELE** *except*

(A) Amy Winehouse

(B) Leona Lewis

(C) Katy B

(D) Kate Bush

When Bob Dylan appeared in a television commercial for **VICTORIA'S SECRET**, which song was he singing?

(A) "Lay, Lady, Lay"

(B) "The Man in Me"

(C) "Love Sick"

(D) "Visions of Johanna"

(E) "Things Have Changed"

Answer: (C) "Love Sick"

Which room in **GRACELAND** was used
as a recording studio?

(A) The racquetball court

(B) The bathroom

(C) The "Jungle Room"

(D) The living room

Answer: (C) The "Jungle Room," which featured a tiki theme,
an indoor waterfall and a green shag carpet. It was
converted into a makeshift recording studio in 1976
so he could record his final two albums.

"Don't wanna be a fool for you/Just another player in your game for two." Who is **SINGING**, and what are they singing about?

(A) Justin Timberlake, about Britney Spears

(B) Backstreet Boys, about a girl who didn't want it that way

(C) Britney Spears, about her mom

(D) 'N Sync, about Lou Pearlman

Answer: (D) 'N Sync, Lou Pearlman. It's from 2000's "Bye Bye Bye," released after the band had severed ties with its manager.

Why was **JAY-Z** pulled over in "99 Problems,"
according to the police officer?

(A) He was missing a taillight

(B) He was doing 55 miles per hour
in a 54-mile-per-hour zone

(C) His music was too loud

(D) The officer wanted a better look
at Beyoncé

In **PULP FICTION**, which song do Uma Thurman and John Travolta dance to at Jack Rabbit Slim's?

(A) "Shout," by the Isley Brothers

(B) "You Never Can Tell," by Chuck Berry

(C) "Carol," by Chuck Berry

(D) "Hound Dog," by Elvis Presley

Answer: (B) "You Never Can Tell," Chuck Berry

Which rocker said that his epitaph should read, "Died. Said '**FIST FUCK**.' Won a Grammy"?

(A) Billy Corgan

(B) Trent Reznor

(C) Perry Farrell

(D) Marilyn Manson

Answer: (B) Trent Reznor. He said "fist fuck" in the song "Wish," and won Grammys in 1993 and 1996.

61

What is the only song by an **AMERICAN ARTIST** to top the U.S. charts in the first five months of 1964?

(A) "It's My Party," Lesley Gore

(B) "I Get Around," the Beach Boys

(C) "My Guy," Mary Wells

(D) "Hello Dolly," Louis Armstrong

Answer: (A) "It's My Party," Lesley Gore

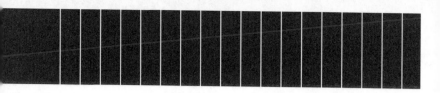

When Elvis visited **RICHARD NIXON** in the White House, his gift to the president was

(A) A gold record

(B) A guitar

(C) A pistol

(D) A white jumpsuit

Answer: (C) A pistol. While visiting Richard Nixon at the White House on December 21st, 1970, Elvis gave Nixon a World War II Colt 45, and Nixon made him an honorary drug enforcement agent.

63

In 1979, Bruce Springsteen debuted "The River" at a star-studded **BENEFIT CONCERT**. The concert was devoted to which cause?

(A) Artists United Against Apartheid

(B) Musicians United for Safe Energy

(C) Vietnam Veterans of America

(D) Amnesty International

Answer: (B) Musicians United for Safe Energy, founded by Jackson Browne, Graham Nash, Bonnie Raitt and others after the Three Mile Island disaster, staged their famous "No Nukes" benefit shows at Madison Square Garden in September 1979.

Shortly after recording **WEEZER**'s 1994 debut album, Rivers Cuomo underwent surgery to correct what condition?

(A) Appendicitis

(B) His right arm was shorter than his left arm

(C) His left leg was shorter than his right leg

(D) His right hand was burned in a fire

Who took **BRIAN WILSON**'s place on the road when the Beach Boys leader stopped touring?

(A) Glen Campbell

(B) David Crosby

(C) Barry McGuire

(D) Sonny Bono

Answer: (A) Glen Campbell

Who was hosting *SNL* the night **SINÉAD O'CONNOR** tore up a picture of the pope?

(A) Joe Pesci

(B) Steve Martin

(C) Tim Robbins

(D) Martin Short

Which of the following artists did trigger-happy control freak **PHIL SPECTOR** (allegedly) *not* threaten with a gun?

(A) John Lennon

(B) Dee Dee Ramone

(C) Leonard Cohen

(D) Ike Turner

Answer: (D) Ike Turner

Which pianist played on most of
CHUCK BERRY's hits?

(A) James Booker

(B) "Piano Red" Perryman

(C) Johnnie Johnson

(D) Otis Spann

All of these words flash across the screen in
Sir-Mix-A-Lot's **"BABY GOT BACK"**
video *except*

(A) STUFFED

(B) BUBBLE

(C) THICK

(D) BUTT

(E) UH

Answer: (D) BUTT

What word appears **20 TIMES** in the 1971 Led Zeppelin track "Rock and Roll"?

(A) "rock"

(B) "roll"

(C) "lonely"

(D) "baby"

We know that on Friday **ROBERT SMITH**
is in love. But how's he feeling on
Monday and Tuesday?

(A) Drab and bruised

(B) Gray and blue

(C) Sad and blue

(D) Broken and used

Answer: (B) Gray and blue

Which **PUNK BAND** advised us to kill the poor, steal people's mail and take a holiday in Cambodia on its 1980 debut album?

(A) The Dils

(B) The Dicks

(C) The Dead Kennedys

(D) The Weirdos

What was the title of **JEWEL**'s
best-selling book of poetry?

(A) *Words in a Mirror*

(B) *Madonna Anno Domini*

(C) *Spokes on the Wheels of a Dream*

(D) *A Night Without Armor*

Answer: (D) *A Night Without Armor*

What did L7's **DONITA SPARKS** throw at hecklers at the 1992 Reading Festival?

(A) A brick

(B) Her tampon

(C) A beer bottle

(D) Her guitar

What is **MISSY ELLIOTT** wearing in the video for her 1997 single "The Rain (Supa Dupa Fly)"?

(A) A jumpsuit

(B) A miniskirt and Timberlands

(C) A trash bag

(D) A golf outfit

Answer: (C) A trash bag

Which song is about the aftermath of a young man jumping off the **TALLAHATCHIE BRIDGE**?

(A) Dusty Springfield, "Son of a Preacher Man"

(B) Otis Redding, "These Arms of Mine"

(C) Procol Harum, "A Whiter Shade of Pale"

(D) Bobbie Gentry, "Ode to Billie Joe"

Which member of **THE MARX BROTHERS**
attended the 1974 launch party for
Led Zeppelin's Swan Song label?

(A) Chico

(B) Zeppo

(C) Groucho

(D) Harpo

Answer: (C) Groucho. The band invited stars like Warren
Beatty and Robert Redford but had to make do with
Lloyd Bridges and Groucho Marx.

Which of the following acts was not produced
by **GAMBLE AND HUFF** for the
Philadelphia International label?

(A) The O'Jays

(B) Harold Melvin and the Blue Notes

(C) Sister Sledge

(D) Teddy Pendergrass

Where does the word "**BONNAROO**"
come from?

(A) It's New Orleans slang for "a really good time"

(B) It's the title of a song by Widespread Panic

(C) It's Tennessee slang for a joint

(D) It's a brand of djembe popular with hippies

(E) It's a nonsense word made up by festival organizer
Dave Matthews when planning the first Bonnaroo

Answer: (A) It's New Orleans slang for "a really good time"

Michael Jackson and his then-wife **LISA MARIE PRESLEY** sought to prove their relationship was real by kissing onstage at which 1994 awards ceremony?

(A) The Grammy Awards

(B) The MTV Video Music Awards

(C) The Academy Awards

(D) The American Music Awards

Which song did **FRANK SINATRA** say was his favorite Lennon-McCartney composition?

(A) "Yesterday"

(B) "Imagine"

(C) "Something"

(D) "In My Life"

Answer: (C) "Something" was, of course, written by George Harrison.

Who was *not* a member of original rap supergroup
GRANDMASTER FLASH AND THE FURIOUS FIVE?

(A) Melle Mel
(B) Wonder Mike
(C) Kid Creole
(D) Cowboy
(E) Scorpio

According to **DAVID BOWIE**, "One day in Berlin, Eno came running in and said, 'I have heard the sound of the future.' " Which record did Brian Eno then play for him?

(A) Kraftwerk, "Trans- Europe Express"

(B) Can, "I Want More"

(C) The Sex Pistols, "Anarchy in the U. K."

(D) Donna Summer, "I Feel Love"

When **KEITH RICHARDS** met
Bob Dylan for the first time, in 1966,
what did Dylan snarl at him?

(A) "How does it feel to be a rolling stone?"

(B) "I could write 'Satisfaction,' but you couldn't write
'Mr. Tambourine Man'"

(C) "Pleased to meet you. Hope you guessed my name"

(D) "I thought you'd never say hello. You look like
the silent type"

Which was the first album **STEVIE WONDER** made after renegotiating his Motown contract, becoming the first artist on the label to win complete artistic control?

(A) *Eivets Rednow*

(B) *Music of My Mind*

(C) *Talking Book*

(D) *Journey Through the Secret Life of Plants*

(E) *Innervisions*

After a string of **COMMERCIAL FLOPS**, which rock star was sued by his own record company for making "unrepresentative music"?

(A) Van Morrison

(B) Bob Dylan

(C) Neil Young

(D) Leonard Cohen

According to **RUN-DMC** in "It's Tricky,"
which of the following is *not* an annoyance of
the rap-star lifestyle?

(A) Long waits at baggage claim

(B) Fans tearing your clothes

(C) People guessing who's in your limo,
despite the tinted windows

(D) Groupies messing with your dad

Answer: (A) Long waits at baggage claim

Neverland Ranch contained a lifesize statue made out of **LEGOS**. Who was it of?

(A) Bubbles

(B) Elvis Presley

(C) E.T.

(D) Darth Vader

Whose sweet tooth inspired **GEORGE HARRISON** to write "Savoy Truffle"?

(A) Pattie Boyd

(B) Ringo Starr

(C) Eric Clapton

(D) Bob Dylan

Answer: (C) Eric Clapton

Which singer did *not* usually
employ **FALSETTO**?

(A) Lou Christie

(B) Del Shannon

(C) Bill Medley

(D) Frankie Valli

Answer: (C) Bill Medley, the deep-voiced half of the
Righteous Brothers, was known for the basso
profundo rather than the falsetto.

91

Which **DECADENT PUNK POET** got Bruce Springsteen to do a spoken-word soliloquy on one of their songs?

(A) Lou Reed

(B) Patti Smith

(C) Nick Cave

(D) Johnny Thunders

Chinese Democracy is the name of **GUNS N' ROSES**' sixth album. According to Urban Dictionary, the term is also slang for what?

(A) The politics of the Bush administration

(B) Cocaine

(C) A promise, often made more than once over an extended period of time that the person is either unwilling or unable to keep

(D) Heroin-addled sex

Which **MARVIN GAYE** hit features studio chatter as background vocals and Gaye tapping out a funky percussion part on a bottle of grapefruit juice?

(A) "Got to Give It Up, Pt. 1"

(B) "What's Going On"

(C) "Come Get to This"

(D) "Inner City Blues (Make Me Wanna Holler)"

(E) "Mercy Mercy Me (The Ecology)"

Answer: (A) "Got to Give It Up, Pt. 1"

Why did the Rolling Stones decamp to **FRANCE** in 1971 for the *Exile on Main St.* sessions?

(A) To allow Keith to get a blood transfusion

(B) To avoid paying British taxes

(C) To get a little sun on the French Riviera

(D) To record in the basement of a famous Parisian brothel

Answer: (B) To avoid paying British taxes. At their revenue level, they'd supposedly have owed 93 percent of their income.

95

DURAN DURAN had three men named Taylor in the band. Which ones were brothers?

(A) Andy and Roger

(B) John and Andy

(C) Roger and John

(D) None of them were related

Answer: (D) None of them were related.

Which of the following is *not* a reason
Bruce Springsteen enjoys being
OUT IN THE STREET?

(A) He can walk the way he wants to walk

(B) He can talk the way he wants to talk

(C) He sees pretty girls passing by

(D) He meets the whores on Seventh Avenue

In "Pride (In the Name of Love)," Bono claims **MARTIN LUTHER KING JR.** was assassinated on "early morning, April four." When was MLK actually killed?

(A) Early evening, April 3rd

(B) Early evening, April 4th

(C) Early morning, April 5th

(D) Early evening, April 6th

Which of the following albums was *not* produced by **TODD RUNDGREN**?

(A) Television, *Marquee Moon*

(B) Daryl Hall and John Oates, *War Babies*

(C) Meat Loaf, *Bat Out of Hell*

(D) Patti Smith Group, *Wave*

Which label signed **LED ZEPPELIN** to a reported $200,000 advance in 1968?

(A) Columbia Records

(B) EMI Music

(C) Atlantic Records

(D) Warner Bros. Records

Answer: (C) Atlantic Records

According to **COLDPLAY**'s "Yellow,"
what do the stars shine for?

(A) You and every dreamer too

(B) You and no one else but you

(C) You and Erykah Badu

(D) You and everything you do

Who are the **SOGGY BOTTOM BOYS**?

(A) The producers behind Lady Antebellum

(B) A Southern-rap quintet featuring Young Jeezy and Slim Thug

(C) The fictional group that sings "Man of Constant Sorrow" in *O Brother, Where Art Thou?*

(D) Bladder-control-challenged characters in a Ween song

Answer: (C) The fictional group that sings "Man of Constant Sorrow" in *O Brother, Where Art Thou?*

Which of these insane and reckless things
did British rock star **PETE DOHERTY**
not actually do?

(A) Get busted for heroin possession as he left a hearing for a driving-under- the-influence charge

(B) Squirt a syringe of blood at a camera crew

(C) Burgle his bandmate's flat in an attempt to get drug money

(D) Allegedly force his cat to smoke crack

(E) Put forth an *Indecent Proposal*-style effort to sell a night of pleasure with girlfriend Kate Moss to a wealthy businessman

Answer: (E) Put forth an *Indecent Proposal*-style effort to sell a night of pleasure with girlfriend Kate Moss.

103

Which of the following songs was *not* written by
JERRY LEIBER and **MIKE STOLLER**?

(A) "Stand by Me"

(B) "Yakety Yak"

(C) "Hound Dog"

(D) "Blueberry Hill"

Answer: (D) "Blueberry Hill"

Which film do the members of **PUBLIC ENEMY** accidentally attend at the end of "Burn Hollywood Burn"?

(A) *Driving Miss Daisy*

(B) *New Jack City*

(C) *Problem Child*

(D) *Dances With Wolves*

What is **AXL ROSE**'s preferred method of payment at the liquor store?

(A) Cash

(B) His credit card

(C) Your credit card

(D) A gun

Answer: (C) Your credit card. Axl makes this confession in the lyrics of the Guns N' Roses song "Night Train."

Which Pearl Jam member did not moonlight in **CITIZEN DICK**, the fictitious Seattle grunge band in Cameron Crowe's 1992 film *Singles*?

(A) Mike McCready

(B) Eddie Vedder

(C) Jeff Ament

(D) Stone Gossard

Name the early **DRUMMER** for
Walter Becker and Donald Fagen

(A) Max Weinberg

(B) Earl Palmer

(C) Chevy Chase

(D) Steve Gadd

Answer: (C) Chevy Chase played with Becker and
Fagen at Bard College, before they started
Steely Dan. Fagen's review: "He was a very
good drummer."

ALLAH AND THE KNIFE-WIELDING PUNKS were an early New Wave incarnation of which disco group?

(A) Chic

(B) KC and the Sunshine Band

(C) The Hues Corporation

(D) The Trammps

Match the nickname with the
E STREET Bandmember

(A) Professor   (1) Clarence Clemons

(B) Phantom   (2) Max Weinberg

(C) Big Man   (3) Danny Federici

(D) Mighty   (4) Roy Bittan

Answer: (A-4), (B-3), (C-1), (D-2)

Who or what inspired the **BYRDS**' tripped-out 1966 masterpiece "Eight Miles High"?

(A) Owsley Stanley

(B) A plane trip to England

(C) A weekend in the California desert

(D) A 3 a.m. conversation with Neil Young

How old was **PRINCE** when he released his debut, *For You*, in 1978?

(A) 13

(B) 17

(C) 19

(D) 23

Answer: (C) 19

Who **HASN'T CO-WRITTEN**
a song with Bob Dylan?

(A) Gene Simmons

(B) Paul Simon

(C) Carole Bayer Sager

(D) Michael Bolton

Who once referred to Elvis' music as a
"RANCID-SMELLING APHRODISIAC"?

(A) Richard Nixon

(B) Leonard Bernstein

(C) Frank Sinatra

(D) Leonid Brezhnev

Answer: (C) Sinatra spoke out against Elvis in 1958. "His kind of music is deplorable, a rancid-smelling aphrodisiac," Sinatra said. "It fosters almost totally negative and destructive reactions in young people." Two years later, Sinatra changed his tune, welcoming Elvis home from his stint in the Army by paying him $100,000 to co-star in a television special.

Which soul diva duetted with
OTIS REDDING on "Tramp"?

(A) Aretha Franklin

(B) Nancy Sinatra

(C) Carla Thomas

(D) Diana Ross

Which member of U2 put up the "**MUSICIANS WANTED**" sign at the Mount Temple Comprehensive School in 1976 that led to the band's formation?

(A) Bono

(B) The Edge

(C) Adam Clayton

(D) Larry Mullen Jr.

Answer: (D) Larry Mullen Jr.

Which signature rock-video move does Simon Le Bon execute in Duran Duran's **"HUNGRY LIKE THE WOLF"?**

(A) He flips over a table

(B) He throws a bowl of rice in the air

(C) He smashes his guitar into a TV set

(D) He rides a motorcycle through a church window

Which **DISTORTION-HEAVY** early British rock scene included Ride and Slowdive?

(A) C86

(B) Paisley Underground

(C) Slowcore

(D) Shoegaze

Answer: (D) Shoegaze. The scene got its name because bands rarely looked at the audience while playing.

Which artist *tied* Michael Jackson's record
of having five **NUMBER ONE** songs
from a single album?

(A) Mariah Carey

(B) Lady Gaga

(C) Katy Perry

(D) Madonna

What was the name of the Greenwich Village tourist trap where **THE VELVET UNDERGROUND** were playing regular gigs when Andy Warhol discovered them?

(A) Cafe Weird

(B) Cafe Bizarre

(C) Cafe Freak

(D) The Yellow Banana

Answer: (B) Cafe Bizarre

What incident precipitated **AL GREEN** becoming a minister?

(A) The shooting of Martin Luther King Jr.

(B) The shooting of drummer Al Jackson

(C) Seeing the O'Jays doing coke in the *Soul Train* green room

(D) Being hospitalized after a girlfriend attacked him with boiling grits

Answer: (D) Being hospitalized after a girlfriend attacked him with boiling grits (and then shot herself; two years later, he bought a church in Memphis and was ordained as a minister.)

121

Which record company executive also scored hit albums by playing trumpet with the **TIJUANA BRASS**?

(A) Ahmet Ertegun

(B) Jac Holzman

(C) Herb Alpert

(D) Tommy Mottola

Answer: (C) Herb Alpert, who founded A&M Records with partner Jerry Moss and scored a Top Five single as late as 1987, "Diamonds," with Janet Jackson on lead vocals. Hey, if you ran the record company, you'd get Janet Jackson to sing on your single too.

What's the name of the character Michael Jackson plays in the **STEPHEN KING**-penned 1997 short film *Ghosts*?

(A) Mystery

(B) Master

(C) Maestro

(D) Magician

Which synth poppers sold out **DODGER STADIUM** for two nights in 1990?

(A) Pet Shop Boys

(B) Depeche Mode

(C) Erasure

(D) New Order

Answer: (B) Depeche Mode

Which group did synth-pop whiz **VINCE CLARKE** found after he left Depeche Mode in 1981?

(A) Haircut 100

(B) Yaz

(C) The Associates

(D) Soft Cell

Which **BEACH BOYS** song was
the most expensive single ever produced
when it was released?

(A) "Good Vibrations"

(B) "Wouldn't It Be Nice"

(C) "Heroes and Villains"

(D) "California Girls"

Answer: (A) "Good Vibrations," Brian Wilson's masterwork, was recorded in 17 sessions over a span of six months, at an estimated cost of a then-staggering $16,000. Despite all the overdubs, engineer Chuck Britz, who was present at the first live take, said the end result sounded the same.

Which **ENGLISH SOUL SINGER** (and former John Paul Jones collaborator) is credited with helping persuade U.S. record mogul Jerry Wexler to sign Led Zeppelin?

(A) Tom Jones

(B) Dusty Springfield

(C) Joe Cocker

(D) Mick Hucknall

In 1999, Britney Spears topped the pop charts with
the song " . . . **BABY ONE MORE TIME**."
How many years would pass before
she repeated that feat?

(A) One

(C) Seven

(B) Three

(D) Nine

Answer: (D) Nine. She did it again with 2008's "Womanizer."

Who has **COURTNEY LOVE** not dated?

(A) Trent Reznor

(B) Edward Norton

(C) Steve Coogan

(D) Oliver Stone

Answer: (D) Oliver Stone. Though she did meet future
former fiancé Edward Norton on the set of
Stone's movie *The People vs. Larry Flynt.*

129

In 1982, **SHALAMAR'S JEFFREY DANIEL** helped set off a dance craze on the BBC's *Top of the Pops*. What move did he bust?

(A) The moonwalk

(B) The electric slide

(C) The Pee-Wee

(D) Break dancing

Answer: (A) The moonwalk

Which celebrity *wasn't* mentioned in
"JAMMIN' ME," the song that Bob Dylan
wrote with Tom Petty in 1987?

(A) Eddie Murphy

(B) Vanessa Redgrave

(C) Joe Piscopo

(D) Debra Winger

Answer: (D) Debra Winger. Eddie Murphy, Vanessa
Redgrave and Joe Piscopo are all people Petty
and Dylan want taken back.

TOOL frontman James Maynard Keenan occasionally acted on which Nineties sketch comedy show?

(A) *Mad TV*

(B) *In Living Color*

(C) *Mr. Show*

(D) *The Kids in the Hall*

Answer: (C) *Mr. Show*

Which of these British Invasion bands was
not from **MANCHESTER**?

(A) Freddie and the Dreamers

(B) Herman's Hermits

(C) Wayne Fontana and the Mindbenders

(D) The Dave Clark Five

Answer: (D) The Dave Clark Five, who were from the London area of Tottenham. The other three groups had consecutive Number One singles on the American charts in the spring of 1965: Freddie and the Dreamers with "I'm Telling You Now," then Wayne Fontana and the Mindbenders with "Game of Love," and finally Herman's Hermits with "Mrs. Brown You've Got a Lovely Daughter."

133

After the Clash kicked out Mick Jones,
JOE STRUMMER made one more Clash album
without him. It was called

(A) *Big Audio Dynamite*

(B) *Cut the Crap*

(C) *No More Games*

(D) *All the Rage*

What was art-rock production guru **BRIAN ENO**'s preferred strategy for breaking creative logjams in the studio?

(A) Flipping a coin

(B) Asking the drummer

(C) Opening a bottle of schnapps

(D) Following instructions written on randomly selected playing cards

(E) Taking everyone out for margaritas

Answer: (D) Following instructions written on randomly selected playing cards, which contained gnomic Eno instructions such as "Abandon normal instruments," "Convert a melodic element into a rhythmic element," and "Get your neck massaged."

135

The Rolling Stones' "Sympathy for the Devil" was partially inspired by which **RUSSIAN NOVEL**?

(A) *Crime and Punishment*

(B) *War and Peace*

(C) *The Master and Margarita*

(D) *The Brothers Karamazov*

Answer: (C) *The Master and Margarita*, by Mikhail Bulgakov

According to Alice Cooper in **WAYNE'S WORLD**, what is unique about Milwaukee?

(A) It is the world's largest exporter of cheese-related products

(B) It has the cleanest water of any city in America

(C) It has elected three socialist mayors

(D) Fifty-seven percent of its residents are of Polish descent

"YESTERDAY" is

(A) The Beatles' first Number One hit in Japan

(B) The first Beatles song to use a harp

(C) John Lennon's least favorite Beatles song

(D) The first Beatles song that has only one Beatle playing on it

Answer: (D) The first Beatles song with one Beatle on it

Which band found its new singer on **YOUTUBE** in 2007?

(A) Styx
(B) Chicago
(C) Journey
(D) Boston

What color was the acid you *weren't* supposed
to take at **WOODSTOCK**?

(A) Orange

(B) Turquoise

(C) Indigo

(D) Brown

Answer: (D) Brown

Which artist's performance at the **MONTEREY POP FESTIVAL** inspired **DAVID GEFFEN** to quit his job as an agent to become a manager?

(A) Janis Joplin

(B) Jimi Hendrix

(C) Jefferson Airplane

(D) Laura Nyro

Which of these things did
MARILYN MANSON *not* do?

(A) Market his own brand of absinthe

(B) Punch a *Rolling Stone* editor

(C) Film himself having sex with conjoined twins

(D) Rip up *The Book of Mormon* on stage in Salt Lake City

Answer: (B) Punch a *Rolling Stone* editor

Which *Off the Wall* song title did Michael Jackson's mother, Katherine, fear was a **SEXUAL REFERENCE**?

(A) "Rock With You"

(B) "Don't Stop 'Til You Get Enough"

(C) "I Can't Help It"

(D) "Workin' Day and Night"

What does **LFO** stand for?

(A) Love for Orlando

(B) Live Fresh Ones

(C) Livin' for Onan

(D) Lyte Funky Ones

How many years were David Coverdale and
TAWNY KITAEN married?

(A) 1
(B) 2
(C) 3
(D) 4

PHIL SPECTOR was responsible for some of the greatest singles of the rock & roll era. Most were big hits, but one of them fared so poorly on the U.S. charts that Spector went into temporary retirement. Today, it's considered a classic. What is this golden-era flop?

(A) "River Deep — Mountain High," Ike and Tina Turner

(B) "You've Lost That Loving Feeling," the Righteous Brothers

(C) "Be My Baby," the Ronettes

(D) "He's a Rebel," the Crystals

Answer: (A) Ike and Tina Turner, "River Deep — Mountain High"

RITCHIE VALENS' recording of "La Bamba" was originally the B side to which single?

(A) "Donna"

(B) "Ooh, My Head"

(C) "Come On, Let's Go"

(D) "Fast Freight"

Which **CHUCK BERRY SONG** did the Rolling Stones cover for their first single?

(A) "Nadine"

(B) "Maybellene"

(C) "Come On"

(D) "Brown-Eyed Handsome Man"

Answer: (C) "Come On"

How much money does **LOU REED** bring uptown to spend on heroin in the **VELVET UNDERGROUND**'s "I'm Waiting for the Man"?

(A) $17

(C) $26

(B) $34

(D) $46

Which song was **SAM COOKE**'s inspiration for writing "A Change Is Gonna Come"?

(A) "Respect," Otis Redding

(B) "Mississippi Goddam," Nina Simone

(C) "Blowin' in the Wind," Bob Dylan

(D) "Where Have All the Flowers Gone," Pete Seeger

Answer: (C) Bob Dylan, "Blowin' in the Wind"

Which **PUNK BAND** titled its live album
The Shit Hits the Fans?

(A) The Replacements

(B) The Dead Kennedys

(C) Gang Green

(D) The Dogmatics

Answer: (A) The Replacements. It was a 1985 live tape of their show in Oklahoma City. According to Paul Westerberg's liner notes, "Our roadie pulled it out of some enterprising young gent's tape recorder toward the end of the night. (Drop us a line, buddy, there's $3.95 in it for you!)"

151

What is former boy-band manager
LOU PEARLMAN doing now?

(A) Co-owning the Orlando Magic

(B) Managing Orlando area rap artists

(C) Serving a 25-year jail sentence for
investment fraud

(D) He's dead

Answer: (C) Serving a 25-year sentence for financial-investment fraud:
Pearlman defrauded investors of over $300 million; he was
also accused of having sexual relations with several of the
underage artists he managed.

Which two U2 members were
BORN IN ENGLAND?

(A) Adam and Larry

(B) Bono and Larry

(C) Larry and the Edge

(D) The Edge and Adam

Answer: (D) The Edge, a.k.a. Dave Evans, was born in 1961 in London; Adam Clayton was born in 1960 in Oxfordshire.

153

Which rapper's biggest hit is referenced in the first line of **PAVEMENT**'s 1992 single "Summer Babe"?

(A) Ice Cube

(B) Vanilla Ice

(C) KRS-One

(D) Eric B.

Answer: (B) Vanilla Ice. The song begins, "Ice, baby/
I saw your girlfriend and she was eating her fingers like
they're just another meal."

What did **BILLIE JOE ARMSTRONG** often wear when performing "American Idiot"?

(A) A *worst president ever* T-shirt

(B) An Army uniform

(C) A dunce cap

(D) A George W. Bush mask

Which DJ received co-writing credit on **CHUCK BERRY**'s "Maybellene," in an early example of payola?

(A) Dick Clark

(B) Murray the K

(C) Wolfman Jack

(D) Alan Freed

Answer: (D) Alan Freed. As Berry put it in his autobiography, "I didn't have any idea that Alan Freed was being compensated for giving special attention to 'Maybellene' on his radio program by a gift from Leonard [Chess] registering him part of the writer's credit to the song. In fact, I didn't know then that a person also got compensation for writing as well as recording a song."

In which Counting Crows video does **ADAM DURITZ**'s girlfriend, Courteney Cox, sit in a dark room and look sad?

(A) "Angels of the Silences"

(B) "A Murder of One"

(C) "A Long December"

(D) "Daylight Fading"

In "**BIG POPPA**," what quick snack does the Notorious B.I.G. require before his rendezvous at the club around two?

(A) A T-bone steak, cheese fries and Gatorade

(B) A Big Mac, two chocolate shakes and a cheesecake

(C) A T-bone steak, cheese eggs and Welch's grape

(D) An arugula salad with goat cheese and a V8

Answer: (C) A T-bone steak, cheese eggs, Welch's grape

Who was **POISON**'s guitarist?

(A) C. C. DeVille
(B) Rikki Rockett
(C) Dizzy Dean Davidson
(D) Snake Sabo

Van Halen's **"(OH) PRETTY WOMAN"**
got banned from MTV for showing

(A) David Lee Roth's full-frontal nudity

(B) A team of strippers streaking through the library

(C) Two dwarfs fondling a transvestite

(D) Alex Van Halen snorting lines off a
nurse's cleavage

Answer: (C) Two dwarfs fondling a transvestite.

Which question was *not* put forth on
THE ZOMBIES' "Time of the Season"?

(A) "Who's your daddy?"

(B) "Is he rich like me?"

(C) "What's your name?"

(D) "What time is it?"

When *won't* they "stone you" in Bob Dylan's
"RAINY DAY WOMEN #12 AND 35"?

(A) When you're at the dinner table

(B) When you're riding in your car

(C) When you're playing your guitar

(D) When you walk all alone

Answer: (A) When you're at the dinner table

Where was **EDDIE COCHRAN**'s taxi headed when he was involved in a fatal car crash?

(A) To the Grand Ole Opry, for a gig

(B) To the hospital, to visit Gene Vincent

(C) To the United Nations, to file a grievance

(D) To the London airport, to fly home to Los Angeles

Which song was *not* written by
BUFFY SAINTE-MARIE?

(A) "The Universal Soldier"

(B) "My Country 'Tis of Thy People You're Dying"

(C) "I Ain't Marching Any More"

(D) "Up Where We Belong"

Answer: (C) "I Ain't Marching Any More" — that was Phil Ochs.

What is the only Beatles song with a "**LENNON-MCCARTNEY-STARKEY**" writing credit?

(A) "Good Night"

(B) "With a Little Help From My Friends"

(C) "Don't Pass Me By"

(D) "What Goes On"

How many times has **BOB DYLAN** performed
at the Newport Folk Festival?

(A) Two

(B) Three

(C) Four

(D) Five

Answer: (C) Four. Dylan played the Newport Folk Festival in
1963 and 1964. But after the tumultuous electric set of
1965 he didn't come back until 2002.

MADONNA's early-1980s band shares
its name with which 1980s movie?

(A) *Pretty in Pink*
(B) *Sixteen Candles*
(C) *Breakfast Club*
(D) *Weird Science*

Which song was co-written by **JACKSON BROWNE** and **GLENN FREY**?

(A) "Doctor My Eyes"

(B) "Desperado"

(C) "Take It Easy"

(D) "The Load-Out"

Answer: (C) "Take It Easy"

"The only fucking **HAPPINESS** that I ever had and then it all gets taken away." Who is speaking, and who are they talking about?

(A) Faith Evans, about the Notorious B.I.G.

(B) Lil' Kim, about the Notorious B.I.G.

(C) Courtney Love, about Kurt Cobain

(D) Dave Grohl, about Kurt Cobain

Why can't the narrator of Bruce Springsteen's
"THE RIVER" find a job?

(A) On account of the economy

(B) They're closing down the textile mill

(C) He got in a little hometown jam

(D) He's got debts no honest man can pay

Answer: (A) On account of the economy

Who did *People* magazine name
"The **SEXIEST ROCKER** of 1998"?

(A) Courtney Love

(B) Gwen Stefani

(C) Kid Rock

(D) Mark McGrath

What did the **ITUNES STORE** celebrate in February 2010?

(A) The entire Beatles catalog finally became available for sale

(B) Its 10 billionth song download

(C) Raising the price of song downloads to $1.99 each

(D) Steve Jobs allowed the store to start selling songs with explicit lyrics

Answer: (B) Its 10 billionth song download

Which **SEVENTIES PUNK LABEL** did
Nigel Dick, the director of Britney Spears'
" . . . Baby One More Time" video, work at?

(A) Rough Trade

(B) Factory

(C) Stiff

(D) Postcard

What was the nickname of the infamously raucous **SUNSET STRIP HOTEL** where Led Zeppelin frequently stayed in the Seventies?

(A) The Riot House

(B) The Shag Shack

(C) The Birdcage

(D) The Golden Tower

Answer: (A) The Riot House, a.k.a. the Continental Hyatt House, where the band members and their entourage were known to toss furniture over the balconies, ride motorcycles through the hallways and entertain groupies in their suites for hours on end.

"Ben," **MICHAEL JACKSON**'s
first solo Number One single, was a love song
addressed to

(A) His brothers

(B) A llama

(C) A pet rat

(D) Ben Kingsley

Answer: (C) A pet rat. The song was the theme for the 1972 horror movie *Ben*, a sequel to *Willard*.

175

Who is **SUKI LAHAV**?

(A) Early E Street Band violinist

(B) Co-writer of "Rosalita"

(C) Bruce Springsteen's biographer

(D) Drum tech on *Born to Run*

Answer: (A) Early E Street Band violinist

What phrase was displayed under **JOHN LENNON**'s name when each Beatle was identified on *THE ED SULLIVAN SHOW*?

(A) "He's the smart one"

(B) "He can't see without his glasses"

(C) "Favorite candy: jelly babies"

(D) "Sorry girls, he's married"

Which of the following **ELVIS COSTELLO** hits was actually written by Costello?

(A) "I Can't Stand Up for Falling Down"

(B) "(What's So Funny 'Bout) Peace, Love and Understanding"

(C) "I Wanna Be Loved"

(D) "Miracle Man"

Answer: (D) "Miracle Man" was written by Elvis Costello.

Who is the only featured guest on
JAY-Z's *The Blueprint*?

(A) Beyoncé

(B) Kanye West

(C) Eminem

(D) T-Pain

(E) Jamie Foxx

Which of the following did *not* belong to the
DEAD-TEENAGER genre?

(A) "Teen Angel," Mark Dinning

(B) "I Will Follow Him," Little Peggy March

(C) "Last Kiss," J. Frank Wilson and the Cavaliers

(D) "Leader of the Pack," the Shangri-Las

Answer: (B) Little Peggy March's "I Will Follow Him," a blast of joyful
jubilation from a 15-year-old singer. Two decades later,
March wrote "When the Rain Begins to Fall," a hit in Europe
for Jermaine Jackson and Pia Zadora.

Which 1980s TV action show did
BOY GEORGE guest-star on?

(A) *Magnum P. I.*

(B) *The A-Team*

(C) *MacGyver*

(D) *Turner & Hooch*

Answer: (B) *The A-Team*. He sang "Karma Chameleon" while Mr. T
rocked out in the audience.

Place these **U2 LIVE** efforts in order
of their release.

(A) *Wide Awake in Europe*

(B) *Under a Blood Red Sky*

(C) *Please: PopHeart Live EP*

(D) *Rattle and Hum*

Answer: B, D, C, A

All these guitarists played on **DAVID BOWIE** records. Which one played the solos on "Fashion," "Heroes" and "Teenage Wildlife"?

(A) Robert Fripp

(B) Adrian Belew

(C) Pete Townshend

What **1997 MUSIC VIDEO** featured
a cameo by Bob Dylan?

(A) "Bittersweet Symphony," the Verve

(B) "Everlong," Foo Fighters

(C) "Good Riddance (Time of Your Life),"
Green Day

(D) "Gone Till November," Wyclef Jean

Answer: (D) "Gone Till November," Wyclef Jean. He briefly
appears in an airport when Jean namechecks him in
the song.

Which **LEGENDARY DIRECTOR** filmed
the recording of the Rolling Stones'
"Sympathy for the Devil"?

(A) Martin Scorsese

(B) Francis Ford Coppola

(C) François Truffaut

(D) Jean-Luc Godard

How old was **STEVIE WONDER**
when he began his recording career?

(A) 9
(B) 11
(C) 13
(D) 15

Answer: (B) 11. His third album billed him as "The 12-Year-Old Genius."

Which member of Led Zeppelin shares a name
with a **FAMED NAVAL COMMANDER**
from the American Revolutionary War?

(A) John Paul Jones

(B) Robert Plant

(C) Jimmy Page

(D) John Bonham

Which single topped the charts in both
1960 and **1962**?

(A) "Hit the Road Jack," Ray Charles

(B) "The Twist," Chubby Checker

(C) "Duke of Earl," Gene Chandler

(D) "Are You Lonesome Tonight?" Elvis Presley

Answer: (B) Chubby Checker, "The Twist"

Which of the following was *not* one of the subliminal messages flashed on a giant screen during U2's **ZOO TV TOUR**?

(A) "Guilt is next to God"

(B) "You're not a racist"

(C) "Everything you know is wrong"

(D) "I want a job, pussy, school"

Which was the first Michael Jackson album *not* produced by **QUINCY JONES**?

(A) *Bad*

(B) *Dangerous*

(C) *HIStory*

(D) *Invincible*

Answer: (B) *Dangerous*

Starting with its **DEBUT SINGLE**,
"It's Too Soon to Know," which vocal group
established the template of the doo-wop sound
(and a vogue for bird names)?

(A) The Falcons

(B) The Orioles

(C) The Penguins

(D) The Flamingos

The percussion parts on **FLEETWOOD MAC**'s "Tusk" were performed in part by

(A) John Bonham

(B) Peter Green

(C) The USC Trojan Marching Band

(D) Billy Burnette

The **GO-GO'S' JANE WIEDLIN** wrote "Our Lips Are Sealed" about her long-distance relationship with an English rock-star boyfriend, using poetry he'd sent her in a letter. Who was the guy?

(A) Terry Hall of the Specials

(B) Mick Jones of the Clash

(C) Dave Wakeling of the English Beat

(D) John Taylor of Duran Duran

Which member of **KID 'N PLAY**
had the high-top fade?

(A) Kid

(B) Play

Which of the following is *not* a **SETTING** in a Bruce Springsteen song?

(A) Near the souvenir stand, by the old abandoned factory

(B) Out at the Trestles

(C) Greasy Lake

(D) In the fields, out behind the dynamo

KC AND THE SUNSHINE BAND
were based in

(A) Cleveland

(B) Miami

(C) New Orleans

(D) London

What was the nickname of the **LUXURY JET**
Led Zeppelin chartered for many
of their tour dates?

(A) Air Force Fun

(B) The Starship

(C) The Mudshark

(D) Carouselambra

RollingStone
ROCK TRIVIA CHALLENGE

Match the Rolling Stone
with his **SOLO ALBUM**

(A) Bill Wyman

(B) Mick Jagger

(C) Mick Taylor

(D) Ronnie Wood

(1) *A Stone's Throw*

(2) *I've Got My Own Album to Do*

(3) *Stone Alone*

(4) *Wandering Spirit*

What was the name of **PETE TOWNSHEND**'s
1982 solo album?

(A) *Two Hearts in the Happy Ending Machine*

(B) *All the Best Cowboys Have Chinese Eyes*

(C) *Empty Glass*

(D) *Got Any Gum?*

Which **BEATLES SONG** is covered on U2's 1988 album *Rattle and Hum*?

(A) "Helter Skelter"

(B) "Here Comes the Sun"

(C) "Lovely Rita"

(D) "Lucy in the Sky With Diamonds"

Answer: (A) "Helter Skelter." In the film, Bono introduces the song by saying, "This is a song Charles Manson stole from the Beatles. We're stealing it back."

Which future soul great co-wrote the 1967
Sam and Dave classic "**SOUL MAN**"?

(A) Al Green
(B) Barry White
(C) Bill Withers
(D) Isaac Hayes

Which band shocked the music industry by scoring a **PLATINUM ALBUM** in 2004?

(A) The Pixies

(B) Sonic Youth

(C) Spoon

(D) Modest Mouse

Answer: (D) Modest Mouse

What Led Zeppelin song was sampled on the 1986 **BEASTIE BOYS** track "Rhymin' and Stealin' "?

(A) "Bonzo's Montreux"

(B) "When the Levee Breaks"

(C) "The Ocean"

(D) "The Crunge"

What did his manager, **COL. TOM PARKER**, say he was going to do after Elvis' death in 1977?

(A) "Find me another Elvis"

(B) "Keep right on managing him"

(C) "Work on my golf game"

(D) "Manage Donna Summer"

Answer: (B) "Keep right on managing him." And that's what he did, until a 1983 royalties lawsuit largely ended his extremely beneficial relationship with the Presley estate.

Which **MODERN ROCK BAND**'s singer
killed himself in 1993?

(A) Gin Blossoms

(B) Collective Soul

(C) Radish

(D) Ned's Atomic Dustbin

If you undid the (real) zipper on the cover **ANDY WARHOL** designed for *Sticky Fingers*, what would you find beneath it?

(A) A photo of a male model in tighty-whities

(B) A pink flesh tone

(C) A Bill Wyman cartoon of a naked woman

(D) The Rolling Stones' lips-and-tongue logo

Answer: (A) A photo of a male model in tighty-whities, who is not Mick Jagger, incidentally.

How many Sex Pistols' recordings does
SID VICIOUS play on?

(A) 0

(B) 3

(C) 5

(D) 10

In which **MÖTLEY CRÜE** song does Vince Neil rhyme "I'd say we've kicked some ass" with "I'd say we're still kicking ass"?

(A) "Looks That Kill"

(B) "Wild Side"

(C) "Kickstart My Heart"

(D) "Girls, Girls, Girls"

Answer: (C) "Kickstart My Heart"

Why does **ROSALITA'S MAMA** hate him?

(A) He skips school

(B) He shoots pool

(C) He rides a motorcycle

(D) He plays in a rock & roll band

What are the **ISLEY BROTHERS'**
first names?

(A) Bill and Ronald

(B) Ernie and Ronald

(C) Ernie and Albert

(D) Dwayne and Bill

Which **ELVIS MOVIE** was his
biggest box-office success?

(A) *Jailhouse Rock*

(B) *Blue Hawaii*

(C) *Clambake*

(D) *Viva Las Vegas*

Answer: (D) *Viva Las Vegas.* The 1964 movie was Elvis'
biggest box office hit, grossing more than
$5 million in the U.S.

211

Which American indie band told its story in
"HISTORY LESSON PT. 2" with the motto
"Our band could be your life"?

(A) The Minutemen

(B) Sonic Youth

(C) Mission of Burma

(D) The Embarrassment

Answer: (A) The Minutemen

In the "**THRILLER**" video, Michael Jackson
tells his girlfriend he's

(A) "A monster"

(B) "Not like other guys"

(C) "Just another Eighties teen"

(D) "Just like other guys"

Which was the first **BRITISH GROUP**
to top the American charts?

(A) The Beatles

(B) The Tokens

(C) The Animals

(D) The Tornadoes

Answer: (D) The Tornadoes, "Telstar." — a 1962 instrumental

Which woman *isn't* referenced in Bob Dylan's
"VISIONS OF JOHANNA"?

(A) Madonna

(B) Louise

(C) Johanna

(D) Mary

Answer: (D) Mary. "Louise and her lover are so entwined," "And Madonna, she still has not showed" and "These visions of Johanna that conquer my mind."

215

In his 1984 **ROLLING STONE** interview, Bruce Springsteen said his acoustic ballad "**STATE TROOPER**" was inspired by which obscure synth group?

(A) Kraftwerk

(B) Suicide

(C) Soft Cell

(D) A Flock of Seagulls

Answer: (B) Suicide

Who said, "I've only written about
200 GOOD SONGS. The rest are B sides"?

(A) Ray Davies

(B) Pete Townshend

(C) John Fogerty

(D) Tiny Tim

Match the Beatle to the **PSEUDONYM**
under which he recorded

(A) John Lennon   (1) Percy Thrillington

(B) Paul McCartney   (2) Ringo Starr

(C) George Harrison   (3) Dr. Winston O'Boogie

(D) Richard Starkey   (4) L'Angelo Misterioso

Answer: (A-3), (B-1), (C-4), (D-2)

What song did U2 contribute to the
BATMAN FOREVER soundtrack?

(A) "Hold Me, Thrill Me, Kiss Me, Kill Me"

(B) "Thrill Me, Hold Me, Kill Me, Kiss Me"

(C) "Kiss Me, Thrill Me, Hold Me, Kill Me"

(D) "Kill Me, Kiss Me, Thrill Me, Hold Me"

When Bob Dylan played the **WHITE HOUSE**, what did he say to President Obama?

(A) "It's an honor, sir"

(B) "How'd I sound?"

(C) "You're taller in person"

(D) Not a word

Answer: (D) Not a word

Which **JOHN FOGERTY** solo hit sounded so much like CCR, his former label sued him for plagiarizing himself?

(A) "Rock and Roll Girls"

(B) "Centerfield"

(C) "Zanz Kant Danz"

(D) "The Old Man Down the Road"

Answer: (D) "The Old Man Down the Road." Fogerty won the case.

221

In **EMINEM**'s "Stan," the deranged fan references which two pop songs?

(A) Phil Collins' "In the Air Tonight" and Eminem's "My Name Is"

(C) Talking Heads' "Psycho Killer" and Limp Bizkit's "Nookie"

(B) Elton John's "Tiny Dancer" and Dr. Dre's "Dre Day"

(D) Aerosmith's "Walk This Way" and Britney Spears' "Toxic"